16.95

D0518212

The Countries

The
Netherlands

Tamara L. Britton
ABDO Publishing Company

Published by ABDO Publishing Company, 4940 Viking Drive, Edina, Minnesota 55435.
Copyright © 2003 by Abdo Consulting Group, Inc. International copyrights reserved in
all countries. No part of this book may be reproduced in any form without written
permission from the publisher.

Printed in the United States.

Photo Credits: Corbis
Contributing Editors: Kristin Van Cleaf, Stephanie Hedlund
Art Direction & Maps: Neil Klinepier

Library of Congress Cataloging-in-Publication Data

Britton, Tamara L., 1963-
    The Netherlands / Tamara L. Britton.
      p. cm. -- (The countries)
    Includes Index.
    Summary: An introduction to the history, geography, people, government, economy,
and social life and customs of the Netherlands, a small country in northwestern Europe
which is famous for its tulips. Includes a recipe for Dutch stew.
    ISBN 1-57765-755-1
    1. Netherlands--Juvenile literature. 2. Netherlands--Description and travel--Juvenile
literature. [1. Netherlands.] I. Title. II. Series.

DJ18 .B75 2002
949.2--dc21
                                                    2001053608

Contents

Hallo!

Hello from the Netherlands! The Netherlands is in northern Europe. It is sometimes called Holland. Its people are the Dutch. Most of the Netherlands's land is flat. Much of it has been recovered from the sea.

Most Dutch people get around on bicycles. But almost all families have a car. Many Dutch people are Catholic or Protestant. But most do not go to any church.

The Netherlands is a **constitutional monarchy**. A king or queen rules the Netherlands and a **parliament** makes the country's laws. Its **economy** is based on service and agriculture.

The Netherlands has a long, proud history. It has suffered through many wars. Today, the Netherlands has a well-educated, **literate** population. The country has a strong economy. The Netherlands's leaders are working to make it a great place to work and live.

Hallo *from the Netherlands!*

Fast Facts

OFFICIAL NAME: Kingdom of the Netherlands (Koninkrijk der Nederlanden)
CAPITAL: Amsterdam

LAND
- Area: 16,164 square miles (41,865 sq km)
- Highest Point: Vaalserberg 1,053 feet (321 m)
- Lowest Point: Prins Alexanderpolder -22 feet (-7 m)
- Major Rivers: Rhine, Maas

PEOPLE
- Population: 15,981,472 (July 2001 est.)
- Major Cities: Amsterdam, Rotterdam, The Hague
- Languages: Dutch, Frisian, English
- Religions: Protestantism, Catholicism

GOVERNMENT
- Form: Constitutional monarchy
- Head of State: King or queen
- Head of Government: Prime minister
- Legislature: Two-house parliament
- National Anthem: "Wilhelmus van Nassouwe" ("William of Nassau")
- Nationhood: 1579

ECONOMY
- Agricultural Products: Cheese, grains, sugar beets, potatoes; cattle, pigs, poultry, sheep
- Mining Products: Natural gas
- Manufactured Products: Metal and engineering products, electrical equipment, chemicals, petroleum
- Money: Euro (1 euro = 100 cents)

AMSTERDAM

The Netherlands's Flag

The Netherlands's euro coin

Timeline

300 B.C.	Germanic tribes and Celts move into the Low Countries
A.D. **814**	Charlemagne dies and the Low Countries are split in two; the Netherlands becomes part of Lorraine
1516	Charles I of Spain becomes king; Spain controls the Low Countries
1555	Philip becomes king; the Reformation spreads through Europe
1568	William of Orange leads the Dutch rebellion
1576	The Dutch gain freedom of religion
1579	Union of Uchtrect unites the Netherlands; Spain attacks
1648	Peace of Westphalia is signed; the Netherlands becomes a free country
1806	Bonaparte claims the Netherlands for France
1813	The Dutch declare independence; King William I rules the Netherlands
1815	Congress of Vienna adds Belgium and Luxembourg to the Netherlands
1830	Belgium rebels and becomes a separate country; Luxembourg rebels
1940 - 1945	German forces occupy the Netherlands during World War II

History

When grouped together the Netherlands, Luxembourg, and Belgium are known as the Low Countries. Around 300 B.C., Germanic and Celtic (KEL-tik) tribes moved into this region.

One of the Germanic tribes was the Frisians. They slowly pushed the Celts across the North Sea into Britain. By the first century B.C., Frisians occupied all of the present-day Netherlands. Then another Germanic group, called the Franks, moved in.

The Franks's greatest king was Charlemagne (SHAR-luh-mayn). He ruled from A.D. 768 to 814. After his death, his empire was divided in half. The Low Countries were also split. Then the Netherlands became part of the French region of Lorraine. The French controlled most of the Low Countries until the 1500s.

Charlemagne

In 1516, Charles I of Spain inherited the land, and the Low Countries came under Spanish control. In 1555, his son Philip became king of Spain and prince of the Netherlands. During this time, Europe was involved in a religious movement called the **Reformation**.

King Philip

During the Reformation, King Philip terrorized Dutch Protestants. He raised taxes and sent Spanish troops into the Netherlands. In 1568, William of Orange led the Dutch people in a revolt. They gained freedom of religion in 1576.

In 1577, the Union of Brussels politically united the Dutch **provinces**. But the three southern provinces remained loyal to the king.

In 1579, the Union of Uchtrect united the seven northern **provinces** of the Netherlands. That same year, Spain attacked. After many years of war, the Peace of Westphalia (west-FAYL-yuh) was signed in 1648. Spain then recognized the Netherlands as a free country.

What followed was a period of world domination. Explorers from the Dutch West India Company sailed the world. They claimed much land for the Netherlands. The company was a leader in trade between Europe, the West Indies, and America.

Signing of the Peace of Westphalia

In 1672, William III became *stadholder*, or governor. In 1689, he and his wife Mary also became rulers of England.

In 1702, King William III of England died. He had no heir (AIR) to become ruler.

So the Netherlands's power declined. In 1806, Napoléon Bonaparte (nuh-POHL-yuhn BOH-nuh-part) claimed the Netherlands for France.

Napoléon Bonaparte

When Bonaparte began to lose power, Dutch leaders again declared independence. In 1813, the Prince of Orange became King William I of the Netherlands.

In 1815, the Congress of Vienna added Belgium and Luxembourg to the Netherlands. Belgium **rebelled** in 1830 and became a separate country. Luxembourg also rebelled in 1830. It finally became an independent country in 1890.

Queen Wilhelmina took control of the Netherlands in 1890. Wilhelmina was a good ruler. She extended voting rights and improved working conditions. She also kept the Netherlands **neutral** in **World War I**.

The Netherlands was not so lucky in **World War II**. German forces invaded the country in 1940. The Netherlands was badly damaged by bombs. Thousands of Dutch Jews were killed in German **concentration camps**.

The Netherlands was liberated in 1945. But war had weakened its **economy**. And the Netherlands gave its colony Indonesia freedom.

In 1948, Wilhelmina's daughter Juliana became queen. Juliana led the country during a time of social change. Drug use was increasing. Many people were getting divorced. And in 1975, the Netherlands's colony Suriname gained independence.

In 1980, Juliana's daughter Beatrix became queen. Beatrix leads a liberal nation. The Netherlands's tolerant social policies and healthy economy make it a great place to work and live.

Queen Beatrix and Turkish president Ahmet Necdet Sezer

The Land

The Netherlands is a country in northwestern Europe. The North Sea borders it on the north and the west. Germany is the Netherlands's eastern neighbor. Belgium lies to its south.

Most of the Netherlands's land is flat. But there are a few uplands. And dunes lie along the North Sea. The highest point is Vaalserberg (VAYL-zayr-bayrk) in the southern Netherlands. It is only 1,053 feet (321 m) above sea level.

For centuries, the Dutch have drained water from the land. The drained areas are called **polders**. The polders lie below sea level near the North Sea. They cover about one-fourth of the Netherlands's land, and contain most of the country's farmland.

The Netherlands has a **maritime** climate. It is mild and wet. The Netherlands gets 25 to 30 inches (64 to 76 cm) of rain and snow a year. The summers are cool and the winters are gentle and mild.

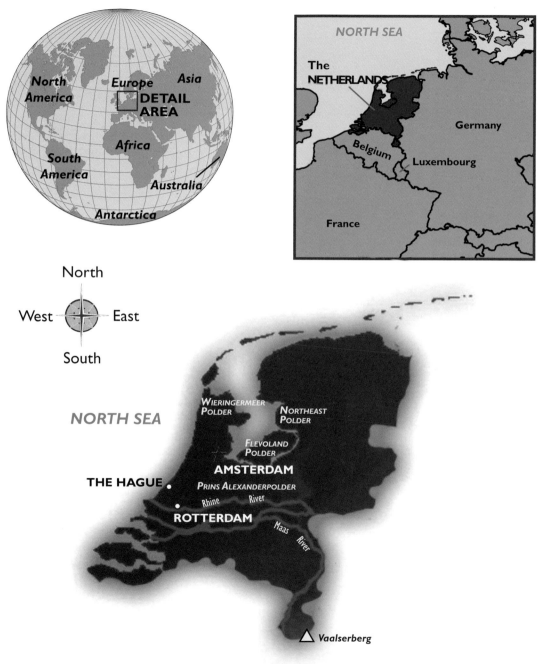

North

West ✦ East

South

NORTH SEA

NORTH SEA

The NETHERLANDS

Germany

Belgium

Luxembourg

France

North America

Europe

Asia

DETAIL AREA

Africa

South America

Australia

Antarctica

WIERINGERMEER POLDER

NORTHEAST POLDER

FLEVOLAND POLDER

AMSTERDAM

THE HAGUE

PRINS ALEXANDERPOLDER

Rhine River

ROTTERDAM

Maas River

△ Vaalserberg

Windmills can be seen throughout the Netherlands. A windmill works when the blades are pushed by the wind and forced to rotate. The rotation produces mechanical power. The Dutch used this power to drain the water from the land, leaving the dry polders.

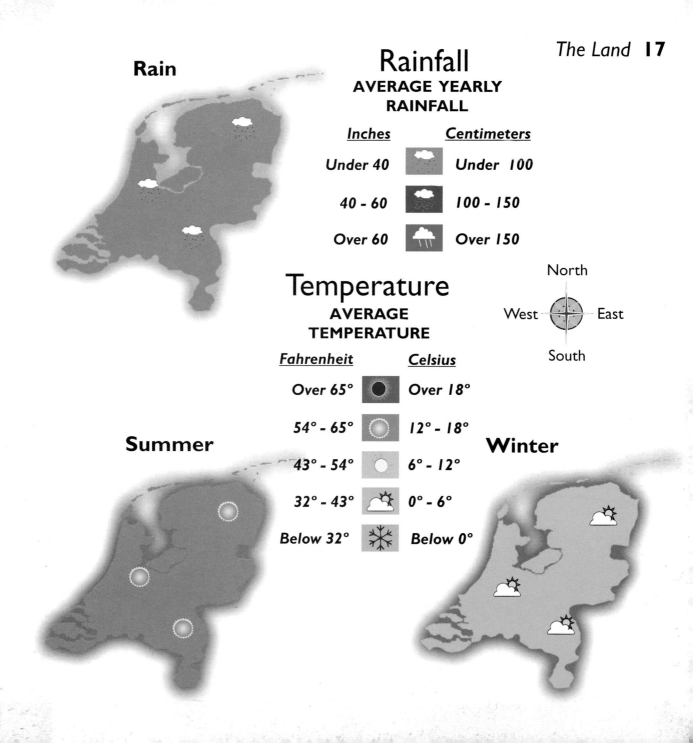

Rain

Rainfall
AVERAGE YEARLY RAINFALL

Inches		*Centimeters*
Under 40		*Under 100*
40 - 60		*100 - 150*
Over 60		*Over 150*

Temperature
AVERAGE TEMPERATURE

Fahrenheit		*Celsius*
Over 65°		*Over 18°*
54° - 65°		*12° - 18°*
43° - 54°		*6° - 12°*
32° - 43°		*0° - 6°*
Below 32°		*Below 0°*

North
West — East
South

Summer

Winter

Wild Things

The Netherlands is a small country. Much of it was covered by the sea. The Dutch people drained the water to provide more land. Today, more than half of the Netherlands is used for farming. So there is not much room for animals to live.

Most of the Netherlands's plants and animals are found in preserved areas and parks. The Dutch began the Amsterdamse Forest in 1934. They planted fir, box elder, maple, and evergreen trees. The last tree was planted in 1970.

Rabbits live in the Netherlands's boggy regions. Red deer and wild boar are the largest animals in the Netherlands. They live in Hoge Veluwe (HO-kay VAY-loo) National Park and are protected by law.

Opposite page: Tulips are displayed at the Keukenhof gardens. The gardens are only open a few weeks each year when the tulips are in bloom.

The Netherlands is known for its tulips. They have become the national symbol. They bloom from March through May. Each year more than a million visitors come to see the Netherlands's red, yellow, and purple tulips. Today, the Dutch export more than six billion tulip bulbs worldwide.

The Dutch

Most of the Netherlands's citizens are Dutch. Many have **immigrated** to the Netherlands from Dutch colonial territories. The largest immigrant group is from Indonesia.

Dutch is the Netherlands's official language. People in the **province** of Friesland speak Frisian. Most Dutch people also speak English.

The Netherlands has no official church. About half of the Dutch population attends Catholic or Protestant churches. But most do not go to any church.

In the cities, people live in apartments or row houses. But single-family homes and farms are common in rural areas.

Today, Dutch clothing is similar to what Americans and Canadians wear. Some people in rural areas still wear the traditional Dutch clothing. This includes full skirts and lace caps for women. Men wear dark, baggy

Opposite page: A woman in traditional clothing carries a tray of herring and bread, a common meal in the Netherlands.

pants and shirts. Most rural people wear wooden shoes called *klompen* (KLOMP-payn).

Many Dutch people eat a light breakfast of bread, cheese, and coffee. Later, they have a light lunch of soup or salad. A common dinner in the Netherlands is fish or meat, potatoes, and vegetables.

Nearly every person in the Netherlands can read and write. Dutch children between the ages 5 and 16 must go to school. The Netherlands has three different kinds of secondary school. One has a general education program. Another has **vocational** training, and the other prepares students for university attendance.

Students may go to a university for five to eight years after secondary school. A university degree is difficult to get and considered a high honor.

Dutch children at school

Klompen, or wooden shoes, are often worn by farmers. They are the most water-resistant shoes in the world.

Hotsput

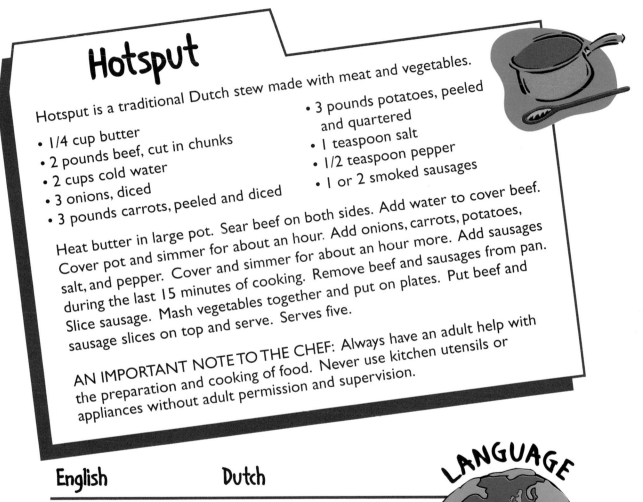

Hotsput is a traditional Dutch stew made with meat and vegetables.

- 1/4 cup butter
- 2 pounds beef, cut in chunks
- 2 cups cold water
- 3 onions, diced
- 3 pounds carrots, peeled and diced
- 3 pounds potatoes, peeled and quartered
- 1 teaspoon salt
- 1/2 teaspoon pepper
- 1 or 2 smoked sausages

Heat butter in large pot. Sear beef on both sides. Add water to cover beef. Cover pot and simmer for about an hour. Add onions, carrots, potatoes, salt, and pepper. Cover and simmer for about an hour more. Add sausages during the last 15 minutes of cooking. Remove beef and sausages from pan. Slice sausage. Mash vegetables together and put on plates. Put beef and sausage slices on top and serve. Serves five.

AN IMPORTANT NOTE TO THE CHEF: Always have an adult help with the preparation and cooking of food. Never use kitchen utensils or appliances without adult permission and supervision.

LANGUAGE

English	Dutch
Yes	Ja (YAH)
No	Nee (NAY)
Please	Alstublieft (ALSTOO-bleeaft)
Thank you	Dank u wel (DONK oo vel)
Hello	Hallo (HAHL-low)
Good-bye	Goedendag (GOOD-an-dawg)

Government

The Netherlands is a **constitutional monarchy**. A king or queen is the head of state. He or she appoints a **prime minister**, who is the head of government. The Netherlands is ruled by the **constitution** of 1814.

The constitution creates a two-house **parliament**. The First Chamber has 75 members. The country's 12 **provincial** legislatures elect these members. The Second Chamber has 150 members that are elected by the people. All Dutch people age 18 and over may vote.

Locally, a commissioner and a council govern each province. The monarch appoints the commissioner. The people elect the council members.

Each province is divided into **municipalities**. A *burgemeester* (boor-gay-MAY-ster), or mayor, is appointed by the monarch to govern each town. A council elected by the people also helps govern the municipalities.

The Binnenhof, in The Hague, is home to the Netherlands's parliament.

Making Money

The Netherlands is a technically advanced country. Its **economy** is highly industrialized. And almost every Dutch citizen is **literate**. But even with these advantages, the country still has some difficulties.

The Netherlands does not have many natural resources. So the country must import raw materials and export finished goods. The Dutch manufacture and export processed foods, electronics, automobiles, and machinery.

Most Dutch people work in the service industry. Financial services such as financial planning, insurance, and real estate make up the biggest part of this industry. Other service related jobs include restaurant, hotel, and trade positions.

Tourism is an important part of the Dutch economy. More than five million people visit the Netherlands each year.

More than half of the Netherlands is farmland. Dutch farmers grow barley, potatoes, sugar bects, and wheat. Dairy farming is the country's most important agricultural industry. The Netherlands is one of the world's major cheese producers. Dutch farmers also raise cattle, pigs, poultry, and sheep.

Cheese is an important part of the economy. People come from around the world to buy the Netherlands's cheeses.

Splendid Cities

Amsterdam is the Netherlands's largest city. It occupies about 90 islands. The islands are connected by about 1,000 bridges. More than one million people live in Amsterdam. It is the Netherlands's capital and financial center.

Rotterdam is the Netherlands's second-largest city. Its population is also about one million. Rotterdam began as a fishing village and became a major port. It is now the largest grain and general cargo harbor in Europe.

The Hague (HAYG) is the Netherlands's third-largest city. About 700,000 people live there. It is the seat of government. Many companies also have their corporate offices at The Hague. Because of this, there is little industry. But the city has many museums and parks.

Rotterdam is the largest port in Europe.

Getting Around

The Netherlands has a vast network of paved roads. Most Dutch families own a car. But gas is expensive. Places in cities and towns are also close together. So bicycles are still the Netherlands's major form of transportation.

The Netherlands has many rivers and canals. Much of the country's freight moves along these waterways. Rotterdam's port is the busiest in the world. It connects much of Europe by way of the Rhine River.

The country's main airport is outside Amsterdam. The Royal Dutch Airlines (KLM) is headquartered there. KLM is the world's oldest airline.

The Dutch also travel by train. Trains leave Dutch stations every half hour. Because the Netherlands is so small, the longest train ride takes less than three hours.

Opposite page: There are more bicycles than people in the Netherlands. More than 16 million bicycles are registered to about 15 million Dutch residents.

On Holiday

The Dutch celebrate many holidays and festivals. Tourists from around the world travel to the Netherlands to enjoy these celebrations.

Elfstedentocht (alef-STAY-dayn-tohkt) is usually held in January. It is an ice-skating race through 11 cities. The Netherlands rarely gets cold enough to freeze all of the canals for the race. But when it does, everyone stops work. They either volunteer at the race or watch it.

In February, Dutch Catholics celebrate Carnival. People wear colorful costumes and have big parties.

The Dutch celebrate Queen's Day on April 30. It is former Queen Juliana's birthday. People celebrate with parades, games, and local fairs called *kermis* (KAYRMEES).

In July, the North Sea Jazz Festival is held in The Hague. It is the largest jazz festival in the world.

The Dutch people celebrate St. Nicholas Day on December 6. On this day, Sinterklaas puts gifts in children's shoes. The Dutch also have two Christmas Days, December 25 and 26. On New Year's Eve, the Dutch celebrate with fireworks.

Sinterklaas arrives in the Netherlands.

Sports & Culture

Bicycle riding is a popular activity in the Netherlands. There are many paths along the coast made specially for bicycling.

Since the Netherlands has many rivers and canals, water sports are also popular. People enjoy boating, sailing, and windsurfing in the warm weather. In the cold weather, many Dutch people enjoy ice-skating.

Soccer is the favorite sport in the Netherlands. The Dutch team is nicknamed The Oranje. They have played in the World Cup finals twice.

The Netherlands has given the world many famous artists. Vincent van Gogh and Rembrandt are two famous Dutch painters. Their work can be seen in museums throughout the Netherlands.

The Netherlands is rich in visual arts. There are about 12 professional theater companies in the Netherlands. There are also 18 national museums. The Netherlands is proud of its **culture**.

Ice-skating on the canals of the Netherlands is a common winter activity. The Dutch enjoy the outdoors and many kinds of sports.

Glossary

concentration camp - a camp where political enemies and prisoners of war are held. During World War II, many Jews were sent to concentration camps in Germany and Poland.

constitution - the laws that govern a country.

constitutional monarchy - a form of government ruled by a king or queen who must follow the laws of a constitution.

culture - the customs, arts, and tools of a nation or people at a certain time.

economy - the way a nation uses its money, goods, and natural resources.

immigrate - to leave one country and enter a foreign country to live.

literate - able to read and write.

maritime - affected by the ocean, sea, or large body of water.

municipality - a city, town, or other community having self-government.

neutral - not taking sides in a conflict.

parliament - the highest lawmaking body of some governments.

polder - land that was covered by the sea, but recovered by windmill power.

prime minister - the highest-ranked member of some governments.

province - one of the main divisions of a country.

rebel - to disobey an authority or the government.

Reformation - a religious movement in the sixteenth century. People wanted to reform the Catholic Church. They formed Protestant churches by making these changes.

vocational - of or relating to training in a skill or trade to be pursued as a career.

World War I - 1914 to 1918, fought in Europe. The United States, Great Britain, France, Russia, and their allies were on one side. Germany, Austria-Hungary, and their allies were on the other side. The war began when Archduke Ferdinand of Austria was assassinated.

World War II - 1939 to 1945, fought in Europe, Asia, and Africa. The United States, France, Great Britain, the Soviet Union, and their allies were on one side. Germany, Italy, Japan, and their allies were on the other side. The war began when Germany invaded Poland.

Web Sites

Would you like to learn more about the Netherlands? Please visit **www.abdopub.com** to find up-to-date Web site links about the country's languages and history. These links are routinely monitored and updated to provide the most current information available.

Index